# PREDICTIONS

# The
# Mind-Makers

RICHARD GREGORY

PHŒNIX

A PHOENIX PAPERBACK

First published in Great Britain in 1998 by
Phoenix, a division of the Orion Publishing Group Ltd
Orion House
5 Upper Saint Martin's Lane
London, WC2H 9EA

A CIP catalogue record for this book is available
from the British Library.

ISBN 0 297 81956 9

Typeset by SetSystems Ltd, Saffron Walden
Set in 9/10.75 Stone Serif
Printed in Great Britain by
Clays Ltd, St Ives plc

*In memory of JZ*
*Professor John Zachary Young FRS*
*1907–1997*

*Who saw that knowledge is as important*
*for the brain of the octopus*
*as for our intelligence*

Many thanks to my secretary,
Mrs Janet John, who holds
the Universe together – Super Gluon.

# Contents

# Pretext

*Pretext:* A fictitious reason given in order to protect the real one
(*Collins Concise Dictionary*).

There is only one way to predict the future – reflect from
the past. Histories of nations are written by winners. The
same is true for science, though of course it would be a
mistake to assume that present-day winners will rule the
future.

Science works from observations and experiments, but
as it is not possible to observe or experiment on the future,
predicting is hardly science; yet science is all about dealing
with present problems for future understanding and
benefit.

What we see from looking back is very much dictated by
personal interests and hopes, so predictions cannot be
more objective than perceptions, and value judgements
enter right from the start. This little book will not be an
'objective' account of the present; neither will it represent
today's best predictions for the future. Probably this is
impossible. For better or worse, it will represent no more
than one person's view of current understanding and what
is likely to develop from this partial view of past and
present. No doubt colleagues will disagree with much of it
– especially if their ideas are left out!

Looking backwards to see the future, we may find trends
and assume they will continue, but often this is misleading. Sometimes we can see general principles unfolding,
such as in organic evolution; but this does not predict
future trends reliably, even though since Darwin we know
the principles of natural selection by which we have
developed from past forms of life. Sometimes, however, we
can at least set limits to the possible. Perpetual-motion
machines can no longer be patented, however novel and
ingenious, for we know on very general grounds that none
will ever appear in the future.

Curiosity, imagination, serendipity and planning for the future got man to the moon and robots to Mars – and also found cures for innumerable diseases, and techniques for imaging functions in our brains. Luck too played an important part in these successes. It is remarkable that the key micro-components of computers (transistors) needed for landing on the moon, were not available when the project was announced in 1959. Developments in one area depend on inventions in other apparently quite unrelated areas, and this makes long-range planning and prediction for science almost impossible. Engineers and inventors, indeed industry as a whole, should take much more credit for advances in science. For discovery depends on the technologies of tools and instruments: telescopes, micro-scopes, space probes, computers. There are instruments that deserve Nobel Prizes for what they have discovered with the help of scientists.

We will look at existing brain minds and computer minds to see what is on offer for future robots and ourselves. So this book is called *The Mind-Makers* – a title which embraces 'Mind brains' and 'Robot brains'. For mind is created by these two kinds of machines. This comes as a jolt for those of us who don't like the idea of a machine in our heads, and for those who don't see even glimmerings of mind in computers. 'Mind Computers' might have been a better subtitle than *Robot Minds*, but I wish to avoid the assumption that brains are like present-day computers. This is for the future to decide.

It does seem miraculous that all our experiences and behaviour are due to billions of interconnected brain cells, communicating with each other with minute electrical signals and subtle chemical changes. Francis Crick, the co-discoverer of the structure of the physical basis of life, DNA, justly called this the 'astonishing hypothesis'. Although the hypothesis is accepted as true by almost all brain scientists, it is indeed astonishing that physcial brains create minds and are the seat of the soul.

All interesting science is astonishing. One has only to think of life evolving by natural selection, or the chemical elements being synthesized in stars – the gold of one's ring having come to earth as cosmic dust from an exploding supernova – or the nature of light, to be astonished. But astonishment makes common sense a poor guide and intuitive prediction unreliable. This, surely, is a major reason for stressing the importance of general knowledge of science, for scientists and for the public – though what it will be like to think in scientific terms and so counter-intuitively on everyday matters, is anyone's guess.

# 1    From the Past

**Past:** Completed, finished and no longer in existence (*Collins Concise Dictionary*).

**Consciousness:** The state or faculty of being conscious, as a condition and concomitant of all thought, feeling, and volition; the recognition by the thinking subject of its own acts or affections (*Oxford English Dictionary*).

The universe has generally been seen as alive and intelligent. For most of us now the notion of mind controlling the universe is akin to magic, though we are very familiar with mind in our own heads controlling our behaviour. Brains are made of the same atoms as the stars – and indeed our brain-atoms came from stars – but there must be something very different in brains from the rest of the universe. What is so special that goes on every day in our heads?

Mind has always been a puzzle. It has not been universally associated with the brain. For the Egyptians the brain was too insignificant to be embalmed. The Greeks saw the planets as intelligent beings, wanderers among stars enslaved on crystal spheres – before their lawful paths were laid out through space and time, by the mathematical science of Galileo and Newton in the seventeenth century. This challenged the age-old belief of astrology, that human destiny is linked with the patterns of the planets.

Astrology had to go for experimental science to be possible. Modern science depends on repeating observations and experiments, so far as possible in the same controlled conditions – but this would be impossible in reasonable time if patterns of planets affected matters, for centuries would have to pass before the patterns recurred, for the next trial to be valid. So mind in the visible sky had to be abandoned for experimental science to develop.

Then one kind of magic, mind-making physics to

explain natural laws, died while another was born – our physics-making mind in brains, now created in computers. This emerged from another magic of pre-science – alchemy – which searched for mind in matter. Alchemy was far more than transmuting base metals into gold; it was a philosophy attempting to relate mind to matter, looking for moral meanings in metals and chemical reactions. Thus 'noble' gold was good not only for its value, but because it resists being changed or tarnished. Unfortunately the notion of life as a special kind of matter was deeply misleading, and has not altogether died, as vitalism remains a popular notion. The discovery, in the 1950s, of the physical basis of the DNA code of life served to kill vitalism in biology; yet the ancient idea that life, intelligence and consciousness are given by some special kind of matter remains intuitively plausible for most of us. Science now looks for life processes that might be carried out by different kinds of matter.

There is a great range of *scale* of physiological processes – from atomic structure, chemical reactions and the hydraulics of fluids to the large levers – bones – for the limbs. It seems likely that mind is carried principally by structures of one scale. Or at least theorists generally plump for processes of a particular scale to explain mind. The cosmologist Roger Penrose chooses the very smallest scale of quantum physics for explaining consciousness, suggesting that future fundamental physics may provide the answer. More popular among brain scientists is the much larger scale of the enormously complicated structures of interconnected neurons of the brain. Each nerve cell or neuron is complex, depending on smaller-scale biochemical processes, especially transmitter substances modifying their connections, or synapses. But the general view is that, although very important for the detailed workings, biochemistry probably does not carry the key processes for mind, these being on the larger scale of nerve structures, or nets.

Emphasis on this larger scale frees mind from specific chemistry, and so allows intelligence and even consciousness to arise from quite different materials, such as silicon.

So Artificial Intelligence is free to try alternative ways of achieving intelligence. Even artificial life is not ruled out.

We have already mentioned consciousness several times. It is quite a recent word, not found before the seventeenth century, 'conscious' being older, originally meaning 'sharing knowledge': 'joint or mutual knowledge' as the *OED* puts it. John Locke famously wrote (1690), 'Consciousness is the perception of what passes in a Man's own mind.' More modern is T. H. Huxley's *Science and Morals* (1866):

> We class sensations along with emotions, and volitions, and thoughts, under the common head of states of consciousness. But what consciousness is, we know not; and how it is that anything so remarkable as a state of consciousness comes about as the result of irritating nervous tissue, is just as unaccountable as the appearance of the Djinn when Aladdin rubbed his lamp, or as any other ultimate fact of nature.

The view I shall take, in the last chapter, is close to Sir William Hamilton's (1788–1856): 'Consciousness is a knowledge solely of what is now and here present to the mind. It is therefore only intuitive, and its objects exclusively presentative.'

The modern term for sensations of consciousness – such as red, green, pain – is 'qualia'. It is these that are so hard to see as 'the result of irritating nervous tissue'. Yet it is just this that is believed by the brain sciences.

Traditionally mind was associated with being conscious – though paradoxically unconscious mechanisms and forces have always been used for explaining conscious mind. A few examples will suffice: elaborate Greek automata and string-pulled puppets (hence *neuron*, the Greek for string); eighteenth-century pumps and pipes (suggesting to Descartes that the nerves are tubes) behaviour controlled with taps; forces of magnetism, suggesting to Mesmer hypnotic attractions; powers of electricity, later used with switches in telephone exchanges, suggesting routing of memories and thoughts by such technology; servo-mechanisms, for stabilizing and goal seeking, as in windmills and autopilots; holograms, where parts can represent the whole; digital computers for calculating and remembering; analogue neural nets, which can learn patterns in space and time and recognize patterns even from small parts.

Presumably none of these have consciousness. There were ancient references to emotion in nature – such as rage, in storms of lightning and thunder – but perhaps these were emotions of human-like gods rather than 'physical' nature. No sharp distinction was made between nature and mind with gods in the scene.

Any notion of explaining mind by analogies with machines was rejected by the French philosopher-mathematician, often called the father of modern philosophy, René Descartes (1597–1650). Famously, he abandoned machines for explaining *mind*, though he accepted the recently invented systems of pumps and pipes of ornamental gardens for suggesting how the *body* works. A water-worked automaton in a Paris park suggested to Descartes that nerves are tubes full of fluid with taps for controlling movements; but he saw the thinking and feeling mind as beyond any physical analogies. This splitting of mind from body is the mind-brain dualism which has been the centre of a philosophical battle ever since – over what we are and what robots might become.

Almost all of us still live with the ancient 'default' notion that our bodies and minds are separate. Quite likely this is suggested by seeing ourselves as ghostly images in mirrors. Mirrors are so familiar it is hard to appreciate their wonder, but it is amazing that we see ourselves separate from our bodies, through the glass or deep in the calm waters of the sacred lake. One's image in the mirror is ghostly – half dead, half alive. It is one's criticizing double, one's *Doppelgänger* marking time. Reflections mislead us philosophically into separating minds from bodies.

The opposed notion, that the brain is a mind-creating machine, was expressed by the French doctor Julian Offray de la Mettrie in *L'Homme machine*, in 1748. This idea was much too astonishing for his medical colleagues. He had to abandon his practice in Paris, and leave his country for the more tolerant Holland. La Mettrie objected to

Descartes's 'two substances in man'. More generally, he defended empirical enquiry against philosophy: 'Let us then take in our hands the staff of experience, paying no heed to the accounts of all the idle theories of the philosophers. To be blind and to think that one can do without this staff is the worst kind of blindness.' He concludes:

> To be a machine, to feel, to think, to know how to distinguish good from bad, as well as blue from yellow, in a word to be born with intelligence and a moral instinct, and to be but an animal, are therefore characters which are no more contradictory, than to be an ape or a parrot. ... I believe that thought is so little incompatible with organised matter, that it seems to be one of its properties par with electricity, the faculty of motion....
>
> Let us then conclude boldly that man is a machine, and that in the whole universe there is but a single substance differently modified. ... Such is my system, or rather the truth, unless I am much deceived. It is short and simple. Dispute it now who will.

La Mettrie compared the brain with watches (which was far from convincing) but there were hints of 'mental' machines long before, especially the calculating beads of the prehistoric abacus. Shortly after Descartes's rejection of machines for mind, mechanisms of calculating gear wheels were invented, the first by Blaise Pascal in 1642, the year of Newton's birth. Then Leibniz invented a better calculating machine to help his father with his accounts, for which he was elected a Fellow of the Royal Society of London in 1673.

It took an oddly long time for the penny to drop that a rule-driven unconscious machine can perform 'mental' tasks universally assumed to require intelligence and consciousness. We still speak of 'mental arithmetic'. These first machines were aids, rather than completely autonomous; but Charles Babbage's programmable Difference Engine of the 1820s, though not fully completed, could carry out complex computations without human help. This was widely known and discussed, yet it hardly suggested that the brain might be a machine solving problems – somehow generating intelligence and consciousness.

Mind without consciousness was generally unthinkable. A decisive alternative was suggested by the polymath German scientist Hermann von Helmholtz (1821–94), who described perceptions as 'unconscious inferences'. Helmholtz saw the perceiving of objects, using absurdly limited data from the senses, as requiring intelligent problem-solving for inferring the external object world by unconscious brain processes. If brains can do this, why not man-made machines?

This was a generation before Sigmund Freud's unconscious mind as the seat of human creativity and emotional problems. Though it came earlier, Helmholtz's account appears more modern as it did not evoke an unconscious mind as a mental entity. It suggested, very differently, that perception and thinking work by physical brain processes, to solve problems of everyday seeing and doing that had gone unrecognized as problems needing answers. This paved the way for Artificial Intelligence. The objection was that it allowed people to think of themselves, and other people, as machines without responsibility and so justifying neither praise nor blame. The saving grace was that we are conscious but machines are not. So a battle was started over the status and role of consciousness that is with us still.

Life on earth is full of artificial-looking patterns and designs. Life seems to have evolved through supreme intelligence solving problems still largely beyond science's understanding. Perhaps this intelligence might be criticized as rather slow – it took 4.5 billion years to evolve us – but the results seem worthwhile. Why shouldn't we call the creative processes of evolution intelligent?

It is sometimes suggested that processes of intelligence are like the natural selection that drives evolution. Perhaps ideas (sometimes called 'memes' by analogy with genes) are like varieties of organisms, attacked and selectively killed by rivals for progress to be made. These kinds of ideas are being developed experimentally by Gerald Edelman with his 'Darwin' robots.

Finding intelligences among the stars would be the second greatest discovery. The greatest being understanding what goes on in our heads, especially why and how we are conscious. From being taboo in science, consciousness is now very much *in* for speculation and experiment. Paradoxically we continue to draw analogies from machines for explaining mind, even though the machines are not conscious, and we do not know how they could produce consciousness. Is the secret to be revealed through developing intelligent robots? We will look at this in Chapter 3 after glancing at the brain.

# 2  Brain Minds

**Brain:** The part of the central nervous system that is contained within the skull . . . the seat of the intellect and of sensation (*Chambers Concise Dictionary*).

**Mind:** *a*: The element or complex of elements in an individual that feels, perceives, thinks, wills, and especially reasons. *b*: The conscious mental events and capabilities in an organism. *c*: The organized conscious and unconscious adaptive mental activity of an organism (*Webster's Collegiate Dictionary*).

## Ants and Elephants

Ants have pin-head brains, elephants have brains twice the weight of ours. Yet, one is tempted to say, an ant is more intelligent than an elephant. For insect behaviour is amazingly complicated and they are far from being mere automata. Insects can learn patterns; navigate, even by taking time into account; communicate, with scents and ritual dances. Species of ants and bees and termites build incredibly elaborate palaces and factories for their colonies. How does this compare with elephants, who are thick skinned, slow and lumbering, though with dextrous noses? Surely the sensitive control of the elephant's trunk does not justify their enormous brain.

Perhaps the crucial difference between ants and elephants is that insects do not play, as elephants and children play. And elephants display social awareness, with bonding and grieving. The mother–child bond is very close, sometimes continuing for fifty years. But individual ants are disposable, sacrificing themselves and each other for the colony they serve, as though they are pawns in a game they don't understand any more than chessmen on a board. One might say that elephants, like us, live in soap-operas of concern with the lives of others. This requires what is now called a 'theory of mind', which children need several years to acquire, for appreciating other people and social roles. Is it living in soap operas that needs, and so through natural selection creates, huge brains? It is ironic that we tend to think of TV soap operas as intellectually demeaning.

Much larger than the elephant's, the largest brain there is or has ever been belongs to the blue whale *Balaenopterus musculus* at 6,800 grams, nearly five times the weight of our brain of about 1400 grams. Although we are supposed to be the most intelligent creatures on earth, we certainly do not have the largest brain. The rule is: larger brains are associated with larger bodies – but they are *relatively* smaller in larger bodies. The ratio of brain to body weight of the whale is less than for any other mammal, only 0.00017. The human ratio is the highest of any mammal, at 0.02. Human dwarfs can have brains smaller than a chimp's (which weighs about 435 grams with a brain–body ratio of 0.007) yet humans with a smaller brain have considerable language while chimps have virtually none. Einstein's brain was rather small. This is just the start of endless puzzles that come up when brains are compared.

The human brain looks like a walnut the size of two clenched fists (Figure 2.1).

Each hemisphere controls the opposite side of the body. This may be because the images in the eyes are optically reversed, sideways and up-down – the brain maps following suit to shorten connections between vision and the touch and the motor-control maps, which are upside down. The surface cortex (Latin 'bark' as for a tree) has deep folds, or 'convolutions', which are most marked in the human brain. It is sometimes said that these increase brain size; but this cannot be so, as the greatest possible volume is a smooth sphere. What they do is increase the surface area of the cerebral cortex, which is associated with the 'higher' mental functions. To my mind this is quite mysterious. Why is the surface of the brain so important? Nerves can connect in all three dimensions, yet the brain's surface connections are restricted essentially to two dimensions so richness of interconnections is lost, not gained.

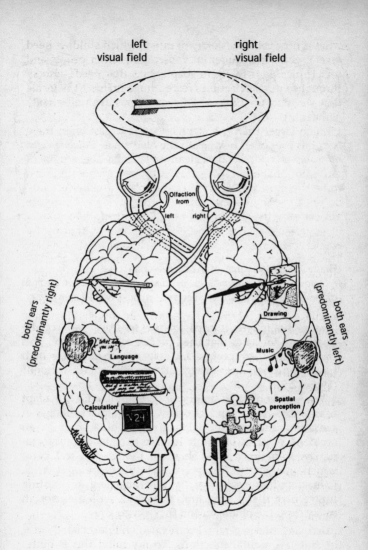

left visual field

right visual field

Olfaction from left right

both ears (predominantly right)

both ears (predominantly left)

Drawing

Language

what did you say

Music

Calculation

√24

Spatial perception

**Figure 2.1 Basic structure of the human brain**
(Nolt (1981), *The Human Brain*, p. 278, Fig. 15–19)

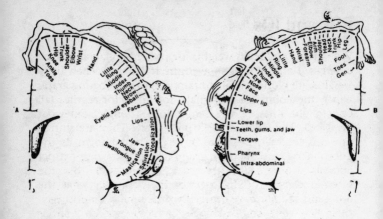

**Figure 2.2 Sensory map of the human brain**
A 'homunculus' – showing areas of sensory cortex for various regions of the body. Brain 'plasticity' allows re-mapping, when a limb is lost.

More brain area is used for the sensitive parts of the body, and for parts that need precise muscle control. This can be shown by homunculi drawings or models, which have corresponding exaggerations like weird cartoons (Figure 2.3).

We now know that brain maps are not fixed. They adapt to new experience, and especially to the radical changes of sensation and control following loss of a limb in an accident. A 'phantom limb' is often experienced (unfortunately, sometimes with phantom though too real pain) which may persist for years. But the neurologist V. S. Ramachandran finds that by superimposing an existing limb where the missing limb should be, with a mirror, in many cases the phantom and the pain go away.

# EQs and IQs

When body and brain weights are plotted on a graph a law emerges. Harry Jerison showed, in 1973, that when body weights are plotted against brain weights on log-log graph paper, the points for mammals, for birds, for reptiles fall on straight lines of the same slope though somewhat displaced. The slope is a 2/3 power law. They are shifted upwards for higher species by a constant known as the Encephalic Quotient (EQ). Extending this to long extinct animals, whose brain sizes can be measured from the internal volume of fossilized skulls, it appears that the dinosaurs did not have especially small brains. Suprisingly, their EQs were comparable to modern reptiles. Man is strikingly above the higher EQ line of the other mammals. This may be associated with the use of tools and our unique development of language.

Why should brain weight be related to body weight, with such a law? Is it possible that early brain design was set by body–brain maps when there was not much else going on in the brain? Conceivably cognitive perception and intelligence is limited by the thin layer of cortex, originally used merely for mapping, so the cortex became folded into deep convolutions to make the surface larger – though a whole dimension of connections is lost through being limited to a surface. This should not limit artifical brains of future robots. They could have huge brains with connections in all directions with small bodies.

The EQ of higher species of vertebrates increases with their intelligence, we might say with their IQ. Particularly heavy individuals must have lower EQs. Can one really increase one's intelligence by dieting?

Brains create minds, but where are minds? Many brain regions contribute. Eighteenth- and nineteenth-century phrenologists thought that individual personality traits and abilities showed up as bumps on the skull – such as a 'bump of intelligence' – due to a specially developed region of the brain containing intelligence; but there is no evidence of phrenological 'bumps' and there is little if any correlation between brain size and human intelligence. This is part of the 'phrenology fallacy'.

It is often thought that losses of regions of brain (from wounds, tumours, operations or special experiments) show where functions are localized. This seems obvious: remove the intelligent bit and intelligence is lost, remove the speech bit and speech is lost – so it should be clear what the various parts of the brain do. But it is not that simple, for in general many functions over many regions are needed for intelligence, or speech or whatever, though the brain is organized in specialized functional 'modules' which can be localized.

Considering the removal of parts from a radio, I wrote, an embarrassingly long time ago: 'Suppose that when [a] condenser breaks down, the set emits piercing howls. Do we argue that the normal function of the condenser is to inhibit howling? Surely not. The condenser's abnormally low resistance has changed the system as a whole, and the new system may exhibit new properties. In this case howling. When a part is removed, the rest of the components may work very differently.' Instead of a radio, one might think of a computer. One has to know how it adds, multiplies, compares and so on, to know or recognise its functions. And brain functions may change, as in an office when someone is away, and others take over the job and work differently.

Such arguments have been seen as challenging the science of neuropsychology. They certainly do not challenge the clinical importance of knowing which bits of brain are crucially important for language, memory, vision, and so on. And the general finding that different regions are important in these various ways has a very general implication: it is strong evidence that *mind is created by brain*. For the different losses of mind resulting from damaged bits of brain make it impossible to believe (though this has been believed for millennia) that the brain is a *receiver* of some external mind. For how could damage to a receiver produce such bizarre particular losses and changes? Clearly the brain *creates* thought, language, emotions and perceptions. These regions are particularly responsible for controlling behaviour and creating experiences. Here perception is most curious for, obviously, the brain does receive information from the external world through the eyes and ears and the other senses, yet it creates a great deal of what seems to be 'out there'. (We discuss this on page 20.)

Losses of even small brain regions can have dramatic effects on experience and behaviour. The neuropsychologist Brenda Milner studied results of operations for epilepsy (in both temporal lobes) carried out by William Scoville in the 1950s. In one celebrated case the epilepsy was cured, but disastrously, for the patient's memory was almost entirely lost. He retained some short-term but almost no long-term memory. Is the problem in learning in recalling, or is the memory store destroyed? Are these given by different brain processes? These are important questions, which are highlighted though not simply answered by such cases.

All experiments need interpreting. What is needed here is understanding of how the brain works, to recognize functions. We simply can't know what a function is without considerable understanding of how the system works. Inferring what normally happens in brains from losses, or other techniques, is particularly tricky because the various parts are highly interconnected and indirectly related to 'outputs'.

# A Paradox of Intelligence

There seems to be a species scale of intelligence, increasing roughly with evolutionary development of mammals – with us on top. But what is intelligence? It might be defined, essentially, as ability to solve problems. But there is something of a paradox. We say that someone who does well by applying knowledge is intelligent; yet we also say that someone who succeeds without using knowledge must be intelligent. If one is intelligent through using, or by not using knowledge, there is indeed a paradox.

The word 'intelligence' has two familiar meanings, the

earlier being knowledge, such as hot news or gossip or secrets of war. This includes 'military intelligence', which does not mean that the military are particularly bright, but that they have special knowledge. This is different from its use in psychology, where intelligence is what is measured by IQ tests.

Measuring human abilities and potentials on a single dimension (like temperature) is worse than inadequate. It is individually and socially damaging, for there is an enormous variety of human abilities and potentialities, which should be respected. We may hope that future research brings richer concepts; recognizing that we are widely different, and that there are many paths to take and ways to succeed. Fortunately there are experts thinking along these lines, notably Howard Gardner.

The Paradox of Intelligence is due to confounding *gaining* with *using* knowledge. It takes intelligence to gain knowledge by learning and discovery; but once it is gained problem solving is often easier. It is a bother for a child to learn the multiplication tables, but once they are learned arithmetic is easier, and more complicated problems can be solved. So a child who knows his or her tables is more intelligent! Yet once they are learned demands on brain processing are reduced, so in another sense *less* intelligence is needed! This is a bit like energy. We may think of working to gain 'potential intelligence' – which can be applied with minimal 'kinetic intelligence' to solve problems. Once potential energy or intelligence is stored, little kinetic energy or kinetic intelligence is needed to apply it. Learning is building 'potential intelligence' for future problem solving with minimal 'kinetic intelligence' being needed.

Is the great variety of human kinds of intelligence – for science, cooking, social skills, music and much more – given by different kinds of knowledge? The difficulty in measuring 'kinetic' intelligence (IQ) is the huge contribution of potential intelligence of knowledge which almost swamps it. Intelligence test questions have to be as knowledge-free as possible, but this is highly artificial.

We are homing in on the enormous significance of knowledge. Is the ant, with its tiny brain, in some ways more intelligent than the elephant with its huge brain, because the ant has inherited directly useful knowledge for its (admittedly somewhat limited) range of problem solving? Does the inherited knowledge of instinct, allow limited kinetic intelligence to work such wonders? I think the answer might be yes.

# Seeing

Whenever we open our eyes in the light, without any apparent effort we see a great richness of shapes and colours and movements of objects lying in external space. This seems easy, but the more we learn about perception the clearer it becomes that seeing involves incredibly clever problem-solving. The flat patterns of light of the optical images in the eyes are somehow transmuted into far richer perceived objects, as things we can use and may harm us. Non-optical properties – hard, heavy, edible, poisonous – are read or inferred from the eyes' images. The visual brain creates a great deal of 'added value' by applying knowledge from past experience to read the present; essentially for prediction allowing survival into the immediate future. Implications of this indirectness of perception are so profound and disturbing, we might call them, following Francis Crick's description of the neuronal basis of mind, the second astonishing hypothesis: that perceptions of vision are psychological projections into outer space. Some of these mind-projections reflect back from the physical world through behaviour as successful or failed predictions. No doubt future robots will do the same.

The visual brain converts the eyes' pictures into something much more like prose – perhaps with a 'brain language' underlying our spoken language and far more ancient. This kind of notion was introduced by the distinguished biologist John (J. Z.) Young, in this way:

If the essential feature of the brain is that it contains information, then the task is to learn to translate the language that it uses. But of course this is not the method that is generally used in the attempt to understand the brain. Physiologists do not go around saying that they are trying to translate the brain language. They would rather think that they are trying to understand it in the 'ordinary scientific terms of physics and chemistry.'

Recent developments in cognitive science are moving in this direction. The techniques of brain scanning are now revealing relations between 'hardware' (or 'wetware') physiology, and cognitive 'software' of the brain. This is the beginning of a very important understanding of how physiology is related to psychology.

The brain creates sensations such as colours which seem to belong to external objects. As Sir isaac Newton appreciated over 300 years ago, light is not itself coloured. Light evokes sensations of red and green, and so on, in suitable eyes and brains. It is brains that create sensations that seem to belong to objects in the external world. Just what is 'objective' and what 'subjective' has confounded philosophers for centuries. The physiologist Semir Zeki, working in London, discovered cells in the brain that generate, or at least are closely associated with, the generation of colour sensations. Colour is 'subjective', created by the brain from various wavelengths of light; yet many sensed properties of objects must be objective. For example a bicycle wheel must be physically circular, as it generally appears (in spite of elliptical retinal images) or it wouldn't work as it does.

# Mind Design

Anatomical descriptions of brain structures are extremely important but we also need to consider many kinds of mental phenomena. These include curious phenomena of vision – especially illusions – which can tell us about both physiology and cognitive processes. They show, when not appropriate, that knowledge and rules can produce illusions. By arguing backwards we can see what these, normally useful, rules are. This can suggest an outline of a mind design. To start, the fact that we are perceptually fooled by an illusion even though we know it is an illusion (and even when we can explain it conceptually) tells us that perceiving and conceiving are largely separate. They are different in various ways. Perception must work within a fraction of a second to be useful; though 'making up one's mind' for conceptual decisions may take minutes or even years. Perceptions are of particular things and situations; conceptions can be general and abstract. Both need knowledge, though rather different kinds of knowledge. So we may put conceptual knowledge in one 'box' and perceptual knowledge in another – connected by a narrow channel as perceptual learning is slower.

The importance of knowledge for seeing shows up when it is lost, as in the visual agnosias. These have recently become well known with the writings of the neurologist Oliver Sacks, especially, *The Man who Mistook His Wife for a Hat.*

# Outline of a Mind Design for Seeing

Seeing starts from what are called bottom-up signals from the eyes and the other senses. After a great deal of signal processing, they are 'read' from top-down knowledge of objects, and from rules introduced as we might say sideways. Thus perspective rules were used by brains for seeing distances and shapes millions of years before artists learned how to use perspective for pictures.

A demonstration of the power of top-down knowledge is the hollow face. Though hollow it appears as a normal convex nose-sticking-out face. This is because convex faces are very familiar and hollow faces extremely unlikely. Knowledge of faces is so strong that it overcomes the bottom-up evidence that this face is truly hollow. Here knowledge dominates, and counters, bottom-up evidence from the eyes.

There are also perceptual instructions for behaviour,

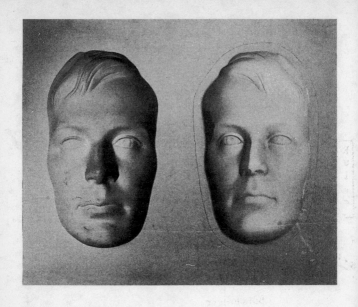

**Figure 2.3 Hollow Face**
The left face is normal. The right face is a hollow mould. The lighting is the same for both. Through the power of top-down knowledge, the right, actually hollow, face looks convex like a normal face.

with feed-back from errors, for learning from mistakes. So we have the beginnings of a mind design for creating Perceptual Hypotheses of the external world, something like Figure 2.4.

Then there is consciousness. It is often suggested that consciousness is an internal monitoring. The philosopher David Armstrong puts it neatly: 'In perception the brain scans the environment. In awareness of the perception another process in the brain scans that scanning.' How sensations are produced by the brain remains mysterious. This is so puzzling that some philosophers try to anaesthetize us into believing there is no problem – no consciousness. So far, I have resisted this philosophical anaesthetics. Though taboo until recently, consciousness is now

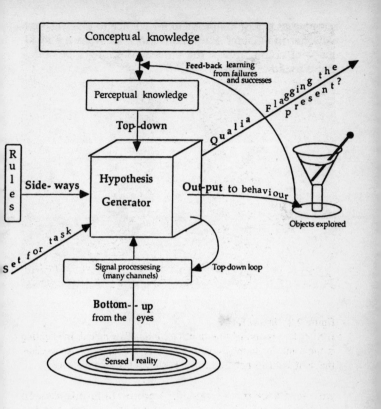

**Figure 2.4  Outline design for the visual mind**
The 'hypothesis generator' is fed 'bottom-up' by sensory data and
'top-down' by stored knowledge. These are shown in two almost
separate boxes: *Conceptual* knowledge being largely abstract and
general; *Perceptual* knowledge of objects making sensory signals,
useful data for perception. General rules (such as perspective and
Gestalt Laws of perceptual organization) are introduced 'sideways'
for reading sensory data. Learning by results of actions, by feedback,
is important. There is some selection of knowledge and rules for the
current task. There are almost certainly 'downwards loops' from the
current perception affecting upwards signal processing.

accepted as a genuine problem for science to investigate. I will offer in Chapter 4 a tentative idea for what the vivid qualia of vision, and of the other senses, might be doing that is useful for survival.

# 3 Robot Minds

**Robot:** *1 a*: a machine that looks like a human being and performs various complex acts (as walking or talking) of a human being; *also*: a similar but fictional machine whose lack of capacity for human emotions is often emphasized. *b*: an efficient insensitive person who functions automatically.
*2*: a device that automatically performs complicated often repetitive tasks
*3*: a mechanism guided by automatic controls. (*Webster's Collegiate Dictionary*).

To create artificial life was a dream of the ancient Greeks, who made elaborate automata of animals and men, and automatic theatres powered by weights sinking through sand or corn and worked with strings, as well as various other wheeled mechanisms of surprising complexity. Elaborate automata were made in eighteenth-century Europe with the rise of clock- and watch-making. Not only paintings and statues, but *moving* statues have a general fascination – from exhibiting miracles to capturing secrets of life in mechanisms. The simple electro-mechanical 'tortoises' of W. Grey Walter, in the 1950s, showed how a simple interacting mechanism can appear lifelike in behaviour.

The word 'robot' first appeared in 1917 in a short story called 'Opilec' by the Czech writer Karel Çapek. 'Robot' became well known from Çapek's play *R.U.R.* (Rossum's Universal Robots), first performed in Prague in 1921 and in New York the following year. 'Robot' is adapted from the Czech *robota*, meaning compulsory labour. The Rossum's Universal Robots factory, on an imaginary island, produced artificial people, with metal skeletons and outer casings, the internal organs being made of ingredients mixed in large vats, spinning wheels producing miles of 'nerve fibre' and 'vein'.

This is a hybrid of two kinds of fictional robots: robots made of people, as Mary Shelley's Frankenstein monster, and simulations of people made of quite different materials, generally with metal brains and no heart. Isaac Asimov's robots are of this genre. Thus Cutie: 'I am composed of strong metal, am continuously conscious, and can stand extremes of environment easily.' It is autonomous robots with artificial brains–minds that interest us here.

Our interest is machines that can see, hear, explore by touch and behave intelligently. Preferably they will be made of non-biological materials. They may not have all our faculties, or facility of thinking and emotional responses, but they must be roughly comparable to humans and to be really interesting they should be in some ways superior. They may have senses beyond ours, such as seeing beyond the spectrum of light received by our eyes, and perhaps added senses such as magnetic, though not, one assumes, 'extra-sensory' perception such as telepathy.

The pioneer of Artificial Intelligence (AI) in the British Isles, Donald Michie, founded the first Department of Artificial Intelligence in Britain in 1967. He anticipated that by the end of the century there would be robot companions, able to do household chores and converse intelligently. Now, almost at AD 2000, this looks further away than it did then. Less ambitious, though extremely effective robots, are however used throughout industry, and for space research. The disappointment is that so far they can scarcely think for themselves.

A useful 'negative' discovery of AI research is its lack of success. This shows how surprisingly difficult it is to see and behave appropriately to various situations – and correspondingly how clever the brain is at solving what are surprisingly hard everyday problems. It turns out that interactive robots need a vast amount of 'common-sense' knowledge which we find so familiar and 'obvious' that its importance for our perception and behaviour was not recognized. It is obvious to us that a cup must be *above* a saucer. We do not need to tell a child this; but a programmed computer must be given such 'common-sense' information explicitly or it will fail, and in human terms look ridiculous. Most surprising is how hard it is to see objects. Vision is usually effortless and seems simple, as its processes are not in consciousness. AI research has shown how wrong this is, which is immensely important for appreciating subtleties of the brain and realizing the difficulties of what it has to do.

Industrial robots are important for assembling cars and so on, but they are not 'philosophically' very interesting as they are computer-controlled with only rudimentary senses, and cannot think imaginatively for themselves. They may well develop into more interesting robots as autonomy becomes commercially valuable. This is dramatically so for robot space probes and planet explorers. It is so because of the delay for communication and control through the great distances of space (two seconds for the moon and eleven minutes for Mars) which makes autonomous intelligence essential for robot space exploration. Surely interesting AI will evolve through these needs, though their autonomy implies lack of control by our descendants.

It is striking how different present-day robots are from living organisms. If and when we have the skills to make humanoid robots, most likely they will still be very different from us simply because humans are not in short supply, and are easily made with a well-proved method by unskilled labour. Their *differences* are likely to be useful to us (as screwdrivers are usefully different from the fingers that we already have). They will, however, have human size and shape when designed to replace humans.

Computers in technology have developed differently from evolving biological brains. Quite simple animals have powers of vision beyond the most sophisticated computer vision; yet a simple computer, costing a hundred dollars, can beat most of us at chess. Computers are good at what we find hard, while we are good at what they find difficult or impossible. Computers have inhuman speed and accuracy yet they are poor at seeing objects, or seeing the point of anything.

More philosophically, computers exist in a mind–matter hinterland. Although their hardware lies firmly in physics (a bit spooky, as quantum effects are important for microchips) their working rules, or algorithms, are not quite physical. Digital computers are powerless without symbolic processes carried out by the physical system. (There is a trap here though: what appear to *us* as symbols may be straightforward causal steps in the machine. For can such machines read meanings in symbols?)

It is important to distinguish two very different kinds of computer: analogue and digital. They give very different suggestions for how brains might work, and they suggest different future intelligent robots.

Digital computers work in physical steps to carry out logical steps. In principle, they can carry out any logical or mathematical operation that can be stated. In practice, in spite of incredibly high operating speeds, they may be too slow. In the 1930s, Alan Turing and Alonzo Church independently proved that digital computers, which they and John von Neuman invented, could in principle perform *any* logical or mathematical operations. But practical limitations, such as speed, are very important for considering artifical intelligence. It no longer seems that digital computing is the way to go. The existing alternative is analogue processing.

Analogue systems are cheap and cheerful, fast and simple, though not completely accurate. They are best for special operations, where speed but not high accuracy are needed, and they can work without having to be programmed. For analogue computers produce answers without having to go through steps of calculations. They avoid having to compute; so strictly it is a misnomer to call them 'computers'. They are analogue *processors*. Perhaps we could call them 'commuters', deriving from the dictionary definition 'to change: commute base metal into gold'. Familiar examples of analogue 'commuters' are slide rules and graphs. Mechanical devices with cams, or electrical circuits such as 'leaky' condensers and non-linear amplifiers, can integrate and differentiate and so on very simply without calculating.

In the 1940s and 1950s it was generally assumed that brains are analogue. Then the rapidly growing power and the flexibility of digital computing persuaded almost everyone that brains must be digital – in spite of the slowness of neurons to change their states as switches for digital computing. Perhaps too the implausibility of suggesting that one's brain had to carry out elaborate calculations even to pick up a cup of coffee, though making heavy weather of a simple sum of long division, made it look unlikely. It is now obvious (if anything is obvious) that neurons of the brain are not suited to digital processing. They are millions of times slower than transistors, and less reliable. But there are many more neurons in the brain than there are transistors in the largest digital computers, and neural interconnections are far richer. The human brain has a hundred billion neurons, each having up to several thousand connections to other brain cells. This is far beyond present-day computers, though this could change within a few years with improving chip technology.

Can computers have minds at all like human minds? Can they be intelligently creative – even to being conscious? Alan Turing, the pioneer of AI and code-breaker of the Second World War, in 1950 suggested a way of comparing humans and computers, by means of the famous Turing Test. The idea was to give a computer and a human (hidden behind screens) the same problems, and get an observer (who would read print-outs from both) to decide which was the human and which the computer. The differences remain great. Computers are far too good at arithmetic, and we are far too good at pattern recognition. Turing's test is a comparison of performances. It does not compare experiences, or have anything to say about consciousness; at any rate while we don't know what, if anything, consciousness does. The Turing Test is too all-or-none. Graded comparisons would be useful. It has been suggested that comparisons of computer with animal intelligence would be suggestive. It turns out that pigeons do embarrassingly well at generalized learning and selecting kinds of features in scenes and pictures.

Turing's Test was a thought experiment but it can be carried out, and indeed is, in the restricted form of computer–human chess tournaments. It turns out that humans and computers are becoming equal at the highest level, though they play very differently. It is easier to make a machine play chess than to make it recognize the pieces on the board.

## Computer Chess

Computer chess started in 1950 with the ideas of Claud Shannon on measuring information. He did this by considering information in a rather simple way, as selecting from a number of alternatives, and defining information in terms of surprise. The more unlikely a message, the more information it conveys. (Pushing this to the limit tells us that extreme surprise is unbelievable. We do and we should doubt another's word, or our own senses, when apparently confronted with a Martian space ship.) This is a matter of pitting the improbability of the message or the perception against the assessed reliability of the source of information. Indeed, if people or computers give highly unlikely messages we deem then unreliable or mad.

Claud Shannon did not succeed in defining meaning. A computer plays chess without understanding the meaning of the positions, or knowing what it is doing. Isn't it somewhat frightening to be beaten in intellectual combat by a 'mind' that is blind to meaning? The chess computers of the 1960s worked by evaluating each position and giving it a 'goodness' number. Moves giving positive numbers for white and negative numbers for black are good for white. White moves to maximize the 'goodness' number – without considering previous actual or future possible moves. After only five moves, there are billions of possible moves that could be made. Searching through all these is beyond the biggest and fastest computer. A program, Chess 4.0, devised by David Slate and Larry Atkin in the 1970s, succeeded in limiting the search to a few million possibilities. The performance got better and better with each speed-up of the computer hardware, until it reached the expert level (2000) in 1979 and the master level (2,200) in 1983. This led to Deep Thought, which in 1988 beat a grandmaster in tournament play. To do this it searched up to 700,000 positions a second. This is hundreds of thousands of times faster than a human brain. The present world-best chess machine, Deep Blue, is a direct development. It can search 200,000,000 chess positions per second. Its heart is a special-purpose chip of over a million transistors, which can search more than two million positions per second. To play chess, several of these special chips are controlled by an IBM SP2 supercomputer. This allowed parallel processing which, however, turned out to be difficult to design, as the results of each parallel computation had to be synchronized. It explores critical moves more deeply. Here it is like a human, occasionally considering sequences up to twenty moves ahead.

How does a human match such superhuman processing speeds? The main hint comes from psychological experiments by the Dutch psychologist A. DeGroot, who compared memory for sensible chess positions with senseless positions, for expert and for run-of-the-mill players. For non-chess positions of pieces, the experts and tyros were much the same, but for sensible positions they were very different. The expert players had apparently superhuman recall of complex positions, viewed for only a few seconds, though were just as 'human' as tyros for non-chess positions. The secret was recognizing meaningful patterns. These become units or 'chunks' for simplifying and speeding up seeing and thinking.

It is suggested that there are as many as $10^{50}$ possible positions in the middle game (that is 10 followed by fifty noughts). Human players rarely consider more than 100 trees for search. Their selection is not arbitrary; it is based on immense knowledge of promising patterns, plus ability to reason, including from known strengths and weaknesses of the opponent – whether human or machine. A grandmaster can play fifty or even more weaker players simultaneously, a glance at the positions selecting up to 50,000 'indexed entries' of their brain's 'chess encyclopaedia', as the AI expert Herb Simon puts it. This looks like intuition, but is really recognizing patterns and recalling appropriate strategies as chunks of knowledge. So the information-processing required is limited, as the work has already been done over years of practice and learning and thinking. (This is vast 'potential intelligence' employed with limited 'kinetic intelligence' as suggested on page 18). Surely it is this that gives meaning for us. But what of computers? When they can build up associations into patterns for 'chunking' thought, won't they also see meaning in the world around them and in their own minds?

## Is 'Hard AI' Impossible?

The American philosopher John Searle has famously challenged the prediction that computers might one day think meaningfully, like human beings. Is John Searle's argument correct? In his 'Chinese Room', Searle considers a Western non-Chinese speaking human helping Chinese people pass symbols of their language, to and fro, in a totally closed room. Searle suggests that the Western person would never discover meanings of the symbols – and that a computer is in the same situation. It *handles* symbols, but without meaning or understanding. We humans get meaning out of computers because we put meaning in and read their symbols in our own terms. According to Searle, this a computer will never do. For him, brains made of protoplasm and developed through organic evolution have meaning and consciousness forever denied to silicon-based (or whatever) components of technology.

The first point that occurs to one is how can a philosophical argument arrive at such a conclusion? Isn't this an empirical matter – coming out in the wash after perhaps hundreds of years of attempts to make intelligent computers? Surely it is a kind of vitalism to suggest that living protoplasm is essentially different in what it can do from any artificial brain. It implies that meaning and consciousness are imbued in special kinds of matter, just as life was supposed by Vitalists to be special-matter-based. This view is now out of date in biology, as more and more physical processes of life are being discovered, especially following the triumph of DNA.

What would happen to a baby brought up in the Chinese Room? Could the baby learn English or any other language if denied related experience? Babies learn by associating symbols with situations and objects, hands on. I conclude that a baby would not extract meanings from symbols in the closed Chinese Room where nothing happens and there is nothing to touch or explore, nothing to relate symbols to reality. This suggests that an active robot with senses and hands might discover meaning in symbols. As babies can do this, why not computer-based active robots?

It will be hard to recognize consciousness in a computer, as it is for animals and indeed for other human beings. This is because we cannot enter or see into other minds. It is also because we do not know what if anything consciousness does. Suppose, at a certain complexity or whatever, computers become creative and make jokes – will we say they are conscious? Such criteria are weak simply because we do not know this for ourselves. We don't know what *our* consciousness does, and we may make a joke *before* appreciating it.

It may be simply too difficult, for uninteresting technical reasons, to create a fully brain-like computer. The chemistry and circuitry of biological brains might be just too subtle to achieve, except by the normal method of reproduction. But I will hazard the guess that it will be achieved, in large part, within a hundred years. Why, though, hasn't an artificial brain already been designed and made?

# A Glance Back to Look Forward

The fullest and most authoritative plan for artifical vision is the work of David Marr (1945–80), who sadly died in his prime. His book *Vision* (1983) describes algorithms for solving the problems digitally. Marr's system works in stages upwards from the stimulus pattern, which is represented in the 'Primary Sketch' in terms of brightnesses for each point or pixel. This leads to what Marr neatly calls a '2½D Sketch' of the basic layout of the scene developed by various stages and processes to complete the representation of external objects. Marr points out that for effective behaviour more than the observer's viewpoint is needed. The brain, or intelligent robot, needs to construct a description of the objects from all viewpoints in order to move around them. This is called 'object centred'. Marr's scheme has stimulated important research, but has not produced an effective working system.

An earlier and very different approach by Terry Winograd was a simulated world of blocks, pyramids and so on, described in words by the computer. It could do this remarkably well, even to coining new words. It had dialogues such as (the computer speaking in capitals):

*'Find a block which is taller than the one you are holding and put it into the box.'*

The system has to figure out what is meant by 'one' and 'it', as well as using deduction to find out which block it is holding.

BY 'IT' I ASSUME YOU MEAN THE BLOCK WHICH IS TALLER THAN THE ONE I AM HOLDING.

There were two possible referents for 'it': the one selected, and 'the one you are holding'. The program has heuristics for choosing between them.

OK

It gets more and more clever, revealing how clever young babies are. It introduces knowledge, inference from knowledge, and guessing and trying out possibilities. It seems (at least to me) clear that a great deal of top-down knowledge is needed for brains and for seeing robots. Our 'common sense' of how things are is very hard to make explicit and feed into a computer. Future AI computers will have to learn for themselves like children – perhaps with neural nets.

# Neural Nets – PDP

Digital computers can be programmed to carry out steps of logical operations, but this does not seem to be how the brain works. The Canadian psychologist Donald Hebb put forward a different scheme in 1949 in his *Organization of Behaviour*, which had a rough ride over the next half-century but now looks like the right approach. Hebb described simple circuits which could learn associations without being programmed or carrying out logical steps. Many such circuits working together are now called Self-Adapting Neural Nets. Revived quite recently by John J. Hopfield and many others, more sophisticated neural nets are coming to be effective learning machines.

Neurons are electro-chemical, with changes of thresholds controlled by chemical concentrations. The connections – synapses – can change conduction with repeated use. So nets of neurons can form patterns of conductivity, representing the external world as internal states of mind. The first artificial neural nets had only two layers, for inputs and outputs. These gave but limited pattern recognition, and for many years the whole idea was almost completely dropped. Then, adding a third, inner, 'hidden layer' allowed nets to generalize abstract patterns and find solutions to general problems. This looked far more brain-like (Figure 3.1). Nets could recognize a learned pattern from only a small part being visible. Like brains, they could go on working, though large parts of the net were destroyed. They were fast, even when their components were slow. They did not need programming – they could program themselves. But just how they work (as they are highly non-linear and interactive) is almost as mysterious as the working of brains. This is annoying for analytically minded neuroscientists who depend on mathematicians – but even they don't pretend to have all the answers.

The key feature is connections changing their conductivity through use. So external patterns, in space and time, produce corresponding internal patterns of conductivities. As we have said above the first perceptron with photo-

35

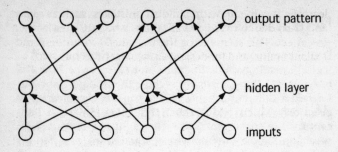

**Figure 3.1 Three-layer neural net, or perceptrion**

electric eyes had only two layers – inputs and outputs. This turned out to be disappointing until an inner hidden layer was added. This – like mind – was related to inputs and outputs and yet separate. It was able to build up abstract generalizations. A neural net of three layers or more can learn to represent objects and sequences of events; it can classify, and it can be activated by just part of the object or pattern it has learned. This is like our recognizing a partly hidden object. As objects often are partly hidden behind other things, this is very useful for biological and for artificial machine vision. A neural net can represent several different (in fact the more different the better) patterns at the same time, and can learn to associate things and patterns, as for learning words and structures of a language. Indeed, artificial neural nets can learn languages, apparently much as children do, starting with babbling and gradually establishing associations between things, or abstractions, with words, and discovering rules of grammar. The mistakes made by nets during learning are revealing. They make the same mistakes as children do with the past tenses of English verbs. Teaching Parallel Distributed Processing (PDP) nets, the pioneers D. E. Rumelhart and J. L. McClelland found, with 400 verbs, some regular, some irregular, that after 190 trials the net was accurate and could respond correctly to verbs it had not already encountered, such as *kept* from *keep*, and *clung* from *cling*. During learning it came up with 'childish' mistakes, such as *comed* and *goed*, due to over-generalization, which it later learned to correct. This seems to be the way ahead for understanding our brains, and for designing intelligent robots.

## What of Emotions and Goals?

For humans and surely the higher animals, emotional states and goals for behaviour are important for selecting what is to be learned, and for what is noticed in perception. Whether or not robots come to have feelings of emotion, they could have goals, selective attention and preferences for what is explored and learned, much as we have. By controlling their goals we may steer their development towards our needs. But, as their bodies and needs will be different from ours, 'moral' direction will have to be made explicitly, and with great care, or they will grow out of control – when anything could happen. The best science-fiction writers, especially Isaac Asimov with his Robot Laws, are perhaps paving the way for this brave new world.

We might think that we could simply turn the robots off if things go wrong; but this will hardly be so when we come to depend on them. It is already extremely dangerous to switch off computers in hospitals, airports, power plants or factories. We are already largely controlled by computers as we depend on them working properly for much of our day-to-day living. When they crash it can be disastrous. Once robots learn to make decisions based on their knowledge and values we will be living in their world, and may be unable to escape.

# 4  To the Future

**Future:** *1*: The time yet to come
*2*: Undetermined events that will occur in that time
(*Collins Concise Dictionary*).

## To Future Technology

### Net gain

It now seems (as we saw in Chapter 3) that the brain is probably a bunch of interacting neural nets. This has important implications. Nets can function without being pre-programmed; can learn for themselves; and they can make use of partial inputs to 'guess' the whole of a pattern or an object. They work fast even with slow components, and though not perfectly accurate are no doubt adequate for normal perception and behaviour. They can continue working though parts are destroyed; in this respect they are like brains, but very different from digital computers. They may not rival computers for carrying out logical or mathematical operations, but this is not what the brain is generally about. Indeed, digital programmed computers are so useful because they are not like brains, which we already have.

In Chapter 2, we discussed problems of localizing functions. This is particularly interesting for artificial or brain neural nets, as they are highly interactive. There are specific losses of speech or perception with localized brain damage. If verbs are lost, or words, for example, referring to fruit, one might think this shows that categories of verbs or fruit words and so on are represented in specific regions of the brain. But how could this be so if brains are interacting neural nets? Experiments involving deliberate damage to artifical nets are revealing, as the damaged net behaves like a damaged brain. It seems that there are two routes for written language: graphic (letter positions of words) and semantic (meanings of words). Damage to either route can produce characteristic confusions of spellings or meanings. An explanation is that words in memory are 'attractors', and damage to the brain or net changes local 'neighbourhoods', so that words normally distant in 'semantic space' may become close – and so be wrongly attracted. As the semantic space is multi-dimensional (according to the size of the vocabulary), results can be bizarre indeed. It is striking that similar confusions occur with the artificial damaged net as with brain damage. This is very different from damaged digital computers.

Nets are now being used for diagnosing and finding patterns of diseases. This has recently been done for the Creutzfeldt-Jakob disease, by training a network with thirty-six cases having the disease and thirty-six non-cases. It builds up classes, and can decide which new individuals belong to which of the classes – without theoretical understanding – which has advantages, especially when our theories are not adequate or correct.

Nets have a great variety of uses, from detecting faults on assembly lines, medical abnormalities to classifying Active Optics for deliberately distorting mirrors to compensate for turbulence of the atmosphere for astronomical telescopes. They are also, of course, used in robot research. The indication is that PDP nets will achieve language recognition and speech with meaning, though how consciousness enters this scene is not clear.

A major problem is how to make a machine that can think in unrestricted situations – unlike chess. How can relevant data be accessed as needed for the billions of associations in our minds? How are thoughts and actions initiated? We have a great deal to learn from psychological experiments, from recording and imaging brain functions, from brain anatomy and biochemistry and changes with brain damage as well as trying out possible designs with computers. Alone, none of these is adequate so the brain sciences cover many techniques. Philosophers can make useful contributions as there are tricky conceptual problems for interpreting observations and experiments.

A most exciting feature of PET (positron emission tomography) scans of regions of the brain is that changes are observed which are related not only to different inputs (or stimuli) but to internal 'mind' changes of how the inputs are being interpreted. For example, Alex Martin and his colleagues got experimental subjects to look at a simple outline drawing of an elephant, and asked them to think either of the elephant's colour or of how it behaves. When thinking of the colour, regions close to the known colour-processing region, discovered by Semir Zeki, lit up. When thinking of behaviour, regions close to movement processors lit up, though again there was no change of input to the eyes. So now private cognitive brain processes can be monitored. In a moment we will look in more detail at this most promising line of research for the future.

## Brain Waves

Finding different kinds of electric 'brain waves' by electroencephalograph (EEG) is important, though we still have little idea what they mean. The famous 'alpha rhythm' of about 10 Hertz from the back of the brain is believed to be associated with vision, yet some normally sighted people (including the pioneer EEG experimenter W. Grey Walter) have no recordable alpha rhythm. Again, we need to know how the brain works to decide whether it is irrelevant (like the vibration of a car engine), or reveals something of how mind is created by the brain. Evoked potentials, elicited by stimuli, are more interesting, as they seem to follow cognitive processes of recognition and thinking. These are recordings with surface electrodes from large areas of brain. Though recently rather out of fashion, they may become important again. There are also recordings of magnetic effects.

Much more precise local recording is done with micro-electrodes, which have revealed a great deal, especially (as we have said) of how the first stages of the visual system works. Particular neurons become active with particular stimuli, or patterns. Important features, such as orientations of lines, movements, colours and so on, stimulate different sets of neurons, which signal key features for recognizing objects. Deeper in the striate 'visual' area, representations become more general, less linked to positions of features on the retina. It turns out that the visual brain is organized into many more or less separate modules, with retinal 'maps' and special analysers for processing various kinds of visual features. Something of this organization shows up in losses of small regions of brain. Occasionally someone loses perception of movement, suggesting that movement is normally processed in a special module, missing for this individual. There could be other interpretations, but this is backed up by findings from micro-electrode recordings of regions specialized for movement (area V5 of the visual cortex), and supported by functional imaging from brain scans. Many techniques, working in conjunction, are needed.

## Images of Mind in Brains

We have the new techniques of PET scans and MRI (magnetic resonance imaging). Now we can see which parts of the brain 'light up' when processing for seeing, hearing, imagining or whatever. These are wonderful advances. How do they work?

In the 1970s, X-ray computed tomography (now called X-ray CT) was introduced. A beam of X-rays is deviated by different densities of tissue. By combining intensities from many angles, a computer could build up and display three-dimensional structures of the living human brain. This was an entirely new use of computers. PET scans are similar except that they produce pictures as slices through the body or brain from weak radioactivity, given by breathing a short half-life radioactive substance emitting positrons such as fluorine. This is a great development from the much earlier autoradiography – in which slices of radioactive tissue were placed on photographic plates, to give pictures of the distribution of radioactivity. It is now possible to do this harmlessly for the living brain with PET scans.

The latest development of MRI works because the atoms of organic molecules are rather like tiny compass needles, which can be lined up in a strong magnetic field. When pulses of radio waves are applied, the 'magnetic needles' of atoms emit characteristic radio waves – indicating kinds and numbers of atoms, from the positrons (positively charged particles) of their nuclei. These signals are combined, by very clever computing, to form a three-dimensional map showing distributions of key organic substances. The dynamic functional activity of the brain can be recorded by PET and it is becoming possible with MRI to yield more detailed information, as chemical changes are shown. This is called functional or fMRI.

These techniques show which regions of brain are active while someone is seeing, thinking, imagining and dreaming and so on. Many old and new questions can now be answered. But, as for any technique or experiment, the results have to be interpreted, and various assumptions are needed. It can take many years of experimental and theoretical work to justify working assumptions, and remove uncertainties and doubts of what the data mean.

One immediate doubt concerns inhibitory regions, for much of the brain *stops* things happening. Active inhibition should show up in PET scans, but might be confused with positive processing. Again, alternative evidence may be needed. One of the most interesting findings is that much the same regions of brains light up with imagining a scene as with seeing it with the eyes. Dreams are very similar to seeing. So signals from the eyes can prevent as well as cause sensations, and illusory perceptions such as dreams and drug-induced hallucinations. In schizophrenia this control is lost.

How far will these very exciting new techniques go? Regions of activity can be distinguished to a few millimetres of spatial resolution. Time resolution is rather poor – being blurred in time over several seconds. So it is generally necessary to average effects from repeated stimuli, which limits what can be found. Unfortunately it is necessary to take difference pictures – subtracting resting activity from changes occurring in the experimental situation. So regions that are active, and perhaps important, both in the experimental situation and in the resting state, are not shown. Developments of MRI show chemical changes in real time, this technique having the advantage over PET of being non-invasive, as no radioactive substance is introduced. fMRI should have a great future.

Much depends on the increased local flow of blood associated with increased brain activity. This introduces time-lags and other problems, but as this mechanism becomes better understood much new light should be thrown on the chemical basis of mind. A general snag for the patient or subject of the experiment is the claustrophobic environment of the scanner. It is like putting your head in a washing machine, with a rather similar distracting noise. No doubt these snags will be overcome. Open scanners, where the head is not entirely surrounded in the machine, are becoming available. The experts Michael Posner and Marcus Raichle believe that space and time resolution will increase, so that activities even down to single neurons may be recorded – possibly even activity within nerve cells.

Does interpreting brain scans have similar difficulties to interpreting effects of losses of parts of brain? Are there, again, dangers of the phrenological fallacy, of assuming that psychological characteristics (such as intelligence) are localized in specific regions, rather than being given by many widely spaced co-operating brain functions that we may scarcely understand? Clearly there are dangers of this kind. Again we need to understand how the brain is organized, and what its functions are, to read these wonderful brain pictures.

These techniques could not have been predicted even a few years ago (though increased blood flow with increase of brain activity has been known for a century) as essentially new discoveries and inventions in physics and computing were needed. It is such breakthroughs as these that are hard and usually impossible to predict. Simple-minded optimism is not enough. Technology does not always come up trumps – electric batteries are still heavy and inefficient. It is naive simply to be optimistic, yet without optimism science and technology would die.

## Artificial Eyes

Experiments are under way on implanting microchips into retinas of the eyes, or into the visual cortex of the brain, to give sight to blind people. This started with the work of

Giles Brindley in Cambridge in the 1960s. He implanted 180 platinum-disc electrodes on to the surface of the visual cortex of a woman who had lost her sight during the war. The electrodes were stimulated by radio signals from a special cap that she wore containing transmitters. The result was that she could see widely spaced multiple flashes of light in about the right places. This was a suggestive start to giving sight to blind people, but turned out to have severe technical problems, now being tackled by Richard Norman and others. One problem is that such a device must work well before it is worthwhile to a person who is used to lack of sight, so initial experiments are hard to justify. It is now found that implanted electrodes (1–2 mm) work better than surface electrodes, need less current and have less disturbing interactions. Rejection of implanted electronics is, of course, a major problem, but there is hope. It turns out that silicon is one of the least rejected foreign substances. We may expect that signals from small video cameras in spectacles will be processed by microchips, and fed to several hundreds or thousands of electrodes, to give useful vision by perhaps 2050AD.

Another ambitious scheme, being developed in America and Germany, is to implant microchips, powered by a laser, in the retina. Highly sophisticated artificial retinas are being developed by Christof Koch and Bimal Mathur. Called 'neuromorphic sensors', they are closely spaced arrays of light detectors combined with analogue parallel processing. They have many of the biological retina's properties; working over an enormous range of intensities and adapting to changing levels of light. They are a miracle of micro-circuitry. But there are severe problems for implanting an artificial retina without damaging the surrounding biological retina, or it being dislocated with sudden eye movements.

## Repairing Brains

The higher up the evolutionary tree the less are organisms able to regenerate lost parts. This is so especially for brain damage. There is no regeneration for mammalian brain cells. Possibly this has something to do with preserving memory, though of course, memory can be lost by brain damage. We may hope that the future will bring self-repair to human limbs, and to the brain.

Quite promising is the implanting of foetal cells, for example for Parkinson's disease, but are non-biological solutions on the cards? Will it prove possible to implant microelectronics into damaged brains? This cannot be ruled out, though is not an immediate possibility. Conceivably, languages and knowledge might be fed into the brain directly in this kind of way. Conversely – and this can be done from EEG waves – brain signals might control machines, or other people, directly, rather as we switch TV channels with a remote control, but without buttons to press.

This leads to the 'science fiction' of virtual reality by stimulating the brain directly. The present goggles of VR are not satisfactory, for the resolution is poor and there is conflict beween how the eyes are focused (accommodated) and distance signalled stereoscopically in the picture. This gives headaches and nausea and can be dangerous because the effects continue for some time. Conceivably, artificial worlds could be fed directly into the brain, perhaps for all the senses, which has hard to imagine possibilities.


# To Future Understanding

## Future Philosophy

The second astonishing hypothesis (we suggested on p. 19 above) largely derives from Helmholtz's view of perceptions as unconscious inferences. As we expressed it: 'perceptions of vision are psychological projections into outer space accepted as surfaces of objects. These mind-projections reflect back from the physical world as successful or failed predictions.' This applies also to hypotheses of science. We may think of perceptions as in many ways like scientific hypotheses. The most significant difference is that some perceptions are conscious, but hypotheses of science are not conscious. Though, as Helmholtz said, the processes of perception are not in consciousness. The great puzzle is why the end result of these processes can be conscious. Is this for ever unique to *brain* minds?

I see no reason why artificial brains should not be conscious. There is no clear reason why similar processes should not be carried out by other means than those (only partly understood) of the brain's wetware. So I anticipate conscious robots – the problem being to know that they *are* conscious. This is the great conundrum.

## Consciousness

Two 'hard' questions are: first, how does the physical brain produce consciousness? Second, what, if anything, does consciousness do?

Presumably only brains are conscious – not tables or stars. There are many suggested explanations for this uniqueness of brains, though none seems really satisfactory. Perhaps the best answer is that consciousness is an emergent property of some of the brain's processes. (This is familiar in chemistry: combining oxygen and hydrogen gives the very different emergent properties of water.) Which brain processes are involved? Could this be discovered by switching off consciousness with anaesthetics?

Some years ago I had myself slowly anaesthetized by injection with ketamine, while my colleagues carried out various tests for which bits of consciousness went in sequence. Initially vision became extremely 'jazzy', though it still worked surprisingly well. For the first time ever I experienced synaesthesia – seeing flashing coloured lights when my hand was touched. Pain went before touch. The last sense to go was hearing. Wouldn't it be interesting to repeat this (frankly unpleasant) experiment during PET scanning? Would this reveal where processes of consciousness are in the brain? As usual the results would need interpreting with various assumptions, but some interesting progress might be made towards finding out where regions essential for conscious mind are in the brain.

What does consciousness do? If it does nothing, why did it evolve through natural selection? Conceivably, it is a mere 'side-effect' of causal processes; but it certainly *seems* too significant simply to be written off. It is interesting to consider one's behaviour when one is not aware of what one is doing. No doubt regrettably, this can occur while driving a car on 'autopilot'. Then, when something unexpected happens, one is suddenly conscious of the situation. One can drive safely without awareness while nothing much is happening – so limited perception does not entirely depend on being conscious. This is brought out by the recently appreciated phenomenon of blind sight. People with damage to one side of the visual brain can have regions appearing blind, and yet responses can be made to movements, and simple objects can be recognized without consciousness. Blind sight has been extensively studied by the Oxford psychologist Larry Weiskrantz.

## Presence of Mind

Perception depends greatly on top-down knowledge of objects and on general rules, such as perspective for seeing things in depth (Chapter 3). Object knowledge and rules are derived from past experience. Some are no doubt inherited from pre-human species. So perceptions are very largely based on past experience, but, as one realizes while crossing a road, recognizing the *present* is essential for survival. It is vitally important that the present moment is not confused with the past. How is this potentially lethal time-confusion avoided?

For primitive, non-cognitive animals, the present is signalled simply by real-time inputs from their senses. Our present is also signalled by sensory inputs; but for us, these have a relatively much smaller part to play – when there are rich cognitive processes for perception – so they must be distinguished from memories from the past, and also from anticipations of what might occur in the future.

A striking exception is the case of Mr S, described by the Russian neuropsychologist Alexandre Luria, whose memory and imagination were so vivid that he had just these problems. He would confuse memories of traffic lights with seeing them now, which was dangerous. These cases are rare, which is hardly surprising.

Our emotional memories, such as embarrassment, are

qualia-rich. Perhaps this is because there are inputs from the body, evoked by memories of embarrassing situations. These signals are in the present, though the memory is from the past. This is the James-Lange theory of emotion – that feelings of emotion are from bodily sensations, as the body reacts to danger, love or whatever. An implication is that our bodies are very important to our minds, so robots will be different even if they become conscious.

Other exceptions – when we experience qualia without the usual sensory signals from the present – are in dreams, hallucinations of schizophrenia and hallucinogenic drugs. These cut off the senses, so the mind drifts free from the present. Then we are truly 'absent minded'.

Does consciousness indeed serve to recognise the present? Is the present moment really flagged by qualia? It is interesting to compare the qualia of seeing with memory of a scene immediately after the eyes are closed. Surely the vivid qualia disappear as soon as the sensory input ceases. Reversing this experiment – opening the eyes and comparing vision with previous memory – the impact of the visual qualia is very striking, the memory being pale by comparison.

A heavily top-down robot must have the same problem for identifying the present. Presumably this could be done without qualia, but future robot designers will have to take this on board. Wouldn't it be interesting if qualia do turn out to be needed for robots!

There are large blind regions in normal eyes, where the optic nerves exit the retinas. These 'blind spots' are as large as thirty stacked moons; yet, even with one eye closed, we do not see them. Are they ignored, or is the surrounding pattern in the retina used to create what should be in the blind regions? Recent evidence shows that the latter is correct. We create qualia from what 'ought' to be there, so we are not disturbed by seeing great black blobs to the side of the eyes, or with scotomas near the centre of vision. This does not work, however, for things different from the surrounding pattern. One can cut off a friend's head by standing about ten feet away and looking to the side with one eye, for although we know he has a head, object knowledge is not available for this quite low-level brain process.

No doubt robots will have to create such fictions to fill disturbing gaps in signals and reality. As for us, their fictions will never be quite reliable when far removed from available evidence from the present.

There are lessons here for designing intelligent robots, the essential being knowledge of the world. This may be learned from interactive experience with objects and with other individuals. It may be implicit knowledge, which cannot be passed on in words – but intelligent robots will have the huge advantage in that their individual knowledge could be transferred to other robots quite directly. The entire contents of computer minds could be passed on – though apart from recorded words and pictures ours is lost at death.

The notion of transmission of learned knowledge from one genration to the next is familiar to biologists in the doctrine of the French pre-Darwinian evolutionist Jean Baptiste Lamarck (1744–1829). Darwin himself did not entirely reject Lamarck's belief that what is learned can be inherited; but gradually it has become clear that this is not true for living creatures. It should, however, be true and extremely important for robots of the future. They will be 'Larmarckian', though we are not, as they will learn directly from each other, and will pass their implicit knowledge down through robot generations. This should be true for digital robot brains, but perhaps it is not so clear that states of neural nets could be downloaded. Artificial nets are almost as mysterious as our brains, and at least we know something of our own brain 'from the inside' by our conscious experience.

As digital memory and computing have some advantages over analogue nets (especially in being more precise), we may expect hybrid robot brains combining advantages of digital and analogue. If circuits become installed in human brains, we may end up with part-human, part-robot brains – with unfailing memories and superhuman computational and logical powers combined with the simple self-learning and resistance to damage of neural nets.

A potentially significant question is how will robots learn? We can teach them what we know explicitly, but much of our knowledge is implicit – not appreciated consciously. Robots will really take off when they can learn from their own observations. But observing needs a lot of interaction with objects, to discover their potentialities and dangers. So, like us, robots will have to learn 'hands on'. A snag is that much of hands-on experience is misleading, which is largely why science is difficult and counter-intuitive. Our 'default' understanding of the physical world is much the same as for the ancient Greeks. Aristotle formulated prehistoric notions of how objects move (especially the incorrect notion that motion stops when no force is applied) which was accepted until Galileo and Newton in the seventeenth century. The point is that these underlying principles are masked by polluting friction, which prevents much of hands-on experience, from infancy, revealing the way things are. So we have perceptual as also conceptual illusions from misleading experience. This has implications for teaching and learning – for us and for robots.

Schools and hands-on science centres can provide experiences which are not misleading (such as pucks moving on an almost frictionless air table) which reveal important principles first hand. There is also virtual reality, which may present not only laws of our universe, but also imagined alternative worlds. There is plenty of scope here for future education of robots and ourselves. I for one would deplore losing hands-on experience to video and computer graphics. Perhaps computer screens are the terminal disease of mankind!

## Minds as Virtual Machines
There is a key idea that links brain minds and robot minds. This is put forward and expounded brilliantly by the American philosopher Daniel Dennett in his book *Consciousness Explained* (1991). The idea is that mind is a virtual machine functioning in the real machine of the brain or a computer.

As a brain is massively parallel and interactive, while a

digital computer is serial and symbolic, there are significant differences in how they can support 'virtual machine' minds. A digital computer can simulate anything that can be stated, so it can simulate very different natural or artificial interactive neural nets that are not digital but are analogue. Converting these simultaneous parallel processes into a single stream of symbols of a digital computer is very time-consuming, so this is an inefficient use of a computer. Although this is useful for experiments on what nets might do, it is far better to build actual interactive nets – artificial analogue brains. Conversely, it is possible for analogue nets to simulate single-channel digital computers; but, again, this is inefficient. No doubt this is why we are so poor at arithmetic compared with the simplest mechanical or electronic digital calculators.

The suggestion is that mind in the interactive nets of the brain is 'made of rules rather than wires'. Although brains are massively parallel, with millions of channels, human thinking (though with hesitations and deviations) is serial. This serial continuity for thinking is greatly helped by language. While thinking, we talk to ourselves in serial language.

It is our brains' language-driven virtual machines that make us unique in nature. Though depending on ancient biological functions, they are essentially different from the innate mechanisms in our heads inherited from our ancestors. Can we impart this trick into man-made machines?

There are extraordinary differences between humans and any other animals, including our most immediate ancestors. Does the acquisition of language, and the associated 'artificial' uses of our brains, explain the differences? Puzzles remain. Looking back at EQ and IQ, in Chapter 2, we see that the size (or weight) of the human brain does not lie along the development line of other mammalian brains. Uniquely, for any mammal over the last five million years, it took off and became much larger in relation to the body weight than any animal that has ever lived. Is this brain growth associated with the beginning of language? If so, which drove which?

These are puzzles about our origins and our present

relation to nature that are bound to inspire research in the coming centuries – no doubt guided by future robot brains having knowledge-based virtual machine minds.

Dan Dennett seems to think that our sensations – qualia – of visual and other perception are so bizarre that they cannot exist. I am not so sure. Indeed I am sure we have qualia, and I see no reason why robots, with roughly equivalent virtual machines running in their artificial brains, should not share many of our experiences. We will have to learn to live with each other.

If future robots have similar senses and behaviour to ours, they will share many of our perceptual and conceptual illusions. Understanding why this is so, we should be sympathetic to their mistakes and beliefs, and so be generally tolerant, which is a lesson for us all.

We can be optimistic over technological advances in communication and in medicine, including prolonging life, though storing ageing brains in the deep freeze (even using advanced cryogenics) for later treatment does seem a non-starter. Complete human brain transplants are unlikely, though introducing fresh cells might well become important for curing diseases, and even for improving memory. Very likely there will be intimate associations between robot and human brains, including electronics inserted into our heads; so as we age we will become part human, part robot. Whether entire human minds will be transferred to machines – even for immortality – might lie centuries ahead; but we should remember that our bodies are important for our minds, especially for emotional reactions and feelings.

Drugs should become more focused with fewer unwanted side effects, relieving such ills as depression and schizophrenia. Possibly virtual reality will become invasive, even stimulating senses other than sight and sound (reminding us of Aldous Huxley's 'Feelies' of *Brave New World*) to blur even further differences between real life and games. Simulating new possibilities will become ever more important, with new industries, for trying out and living in hypothetical futures, before they are realised or abandoned for creating realities. Indeed, distinctions between fantasy and reality will be blurred even further as simulations and prostheses come to dominate our lives. This will change profoundly art and science, and ourselves as experiencing thinking beings.

The Empiricist philosophers of two centuries ago were wrong to think of perception as passive experience from raw data: now we know that all sensory data are cooked, by interpretations from knowledge and assumptions which will become ever richer, though not necessarily more appropriate, as technology encroaches further into mind. Mind control will become a serious threat. No doubt techniques will develop to give some protection against sinister evil-doers and the more benign advertisers, though it will be hard to maintain our individual integrities. All this is following the road that early man took when homo separated from our biological origins, through language, art and science. So far this has been unpredictable and uncontrollable. Now, with more knowledge and more powerful technologies, there is some chance to steer our course into the future. But there will always be surprises – to keep mind alive and life interesting and worth living – whether we are people or robots.

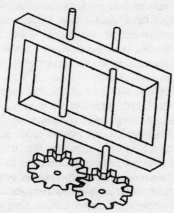

Cogs of cognition

# Further reading

## Chapter 1: From the Past

Dennett, D. (1991) *Consciousness Explained* (Boston: Little, Brown).

Edelman, Gerald (1994) *Bright Air, Brilliant Fire* (London: Penguin).

Gregory, R. L. (1981) *Mind in Science* (London: Weidenfeld and Nicolson/Penguin).

Penrose, R. (1989) *The Emperor's New Mind* (Oxford: OUP).

Westfall, R. (1980) *Never at Rest: A Biography of Isaac Newton* (Cambridge: CUP).

## Chapter 2: Brain Minds

Crick, F. (1994) *The Astonishing Hypothesis: The Scientific Search for the Soul* (London: Macmillan).

Desimone, R. and Ungerleider, L. G. (1989) 'Neural processing of visual information in monkeys' in *Handbook of Neuropsychology*, edited by F. Boller and J. Grafman, pp. 267–99 (Amsterdam: Elsevier).

Felleman, D. J. and van Essen, D. C. (1991). 'Distributed hierarchical processing in the primate cerebral cortex' in *Cerebral Cortex 1*, pp. 1–47.

Gardner, H. (1983) *Frames of Mind* (London: HarperCollins).

Gazzaniga, M. S. (1988) 'Brain modularity: Towards a philosophy of conscious experience' in *Consciousness in Contemporary Science* edited by A. Marcel and Bisiac. (Oxford: Clarendon Press).

Gregory, R. L. (1959) 'Models and localization of function in the central nervous system' in *Mechanization of Thought Processes, Vol. 2* (London: National Physical Laboratory, H. M. Stationery Office), pp. 669–81.

Gregory, R. L. (1961) 'The Brain as an Engineering Problem' in

*Current Problems in Animal Behaviour* edited by W. H. Thorpe and O. L. Zangwill (London: Methuen).

Gregory, R. L. (1987) 'Intelligence based on knowledge – knowledge based on intelligence' in *Creative Intelligences* edited by R. L. Gregory and P. K. Marstrand (London: Frances Pinter).

Gregory, R. L. (1997) *Eye and Brain*, 5th edition (Oxford: OUP).

Gregory, R. L. (1997) *Mirrors in Mind* (Oxford: OUP/New York: W. H. Freeman).

Humphries, G. W. and Riddock, M. J. (1987) *To See but not to See: a Case Study of Visual Agnosia* (London: Lawrence Erlbaum).

Jerison, H. J. (1976) 'Paeleoneurology and the Evolution of Mind' in Readings from the Scientific American: *The Workings of the Brain: Development, Memory and Perception*, edited by Rodolfa Llinàs, pp. 3–16.

Ramachandran, V. S. and Rogers-Ramachandran, D. (1996) Synaesthesia in phantom limbs induced with mirrors, *Proceedings of the Royal Society of London* B pp. 263, 377–86.

Sacks, O. (1985) *The Man Who Mistook his Wife for a Hat* (London: Duckworth).

Young, J. Z. (1978) *Programs of the Brain* (Oxford: OUP).

Zeki, S. (1993) *A Vision of the Brain* (Oxford: Blackwell).

## Chapter 3: Robot Minds

Hebb, D. O. (1949) *Organization of Behaviour* (New York: Wiley).

Michie, D. (1974) *On Machine Intelligence* (Edinburgh: University of Edinburgh).

Turing, A. M. (1950) 'Computing Machinery and Intelligence', Mind, 59, pp. 433–60. (Reprinted in *Computation and Intelligence* edited by G. F. Luger (1996) (Cambridge Mass: MIT Press.)

## Chapter 4: To the Future

Gregory, R. L. (1986) 'Journey into Unconsciousness with Ketamine' in *Odd Perceptions* (London: Methuen).

Hinton, G. E., Plaut D. C., Shallice T. (1993) 'Simulation Brain Damage', *Scientific American*, 269, 4, pp. 76–82.

Luria, A. R. (1969) *The Mind of a Mnemonist* (London: Penguin).

Martin A, Haxby J. V., Lalonde F. M., Wiggs C. L., Ungerleider L. G. (1995) 'Discrete Cortical Regions Associated with Knowledge of Color and Knowledge of Action', *Science*, 270, pp. 102–105.

Posner M. J. and Raichle M. E. (1994) *Images of Mind* (New York: Scientific American Library).

Ramachandran V. S, and Gregory R. L. (1991) 'Perceptual Filling-in of Artificially Induced Scotomas in Human Vision', *Nature*, 350, 6320, pp. 699–702.

Weiskrantz, L. (1997) *Consciousness Lost and Found* (Oxford: OUP).